Arctic Animals
Life Outside the Igloo

Harp Seal

by Dee Phillips

Consultants:

Dr. W. Don Bowen, Research Scientist
Bedford Institute of Oceanography, Fisheries and Oceans, Nova Scotia, Canada

Kimberly Brenneman, PhD
National Institute for Early Education Research, Rutgers University, New Brunswick, New Jersey

BEARPORT
PUBLISHING

New York, New York

Credits

Cover, © Ingo Arndt/Minden Pictures/FLPA; 2–3, © Vladimir Meinik/Shutterstock; 4, © Denis Burdin/Shutterstock; 5, © Michio Hoshino/Minden Pictures/FLPA; 7T, © blickwinkel/Alamy; 7B, © Michio Hoshino/Minden Pictures/FLPA; 8T, © Franco Banfi/Seapics.com; 8B, © Rich Carey/Shutterstock; 9, © Brian J. Skerry/National Geographic Creative; 10, © Michio Hoshino/Minden Pictures/FLPA; 11, © Egmont Strigl/Imagebroker/FLPA; 12, © Gerard Lacz/FLPA; 13, © Gabriela Staebler/Alamy; 14, © La Nau de Fotografia/Shutterstock; 15, © Ingo Arndt/Minden Pictures/FLPA; 16, © Michio Hoshino/Minden Pictures/FLPA; 17, © Jurgen & Christine Sohns/FLPA; 18, © Michio Hoshino/Minden Pictures/FLPA; 19, © Jurgen Freund/Nature Picture Library; 20T, © Mitsuaki Iwago/Minden Pictures/FLPA; 20B, © Brian J. Skerry/National Geographic Creative; 21, © Egmont Strigl/Imagebroker/FLPA; 22, © Ruby Tuesday Books; 23TC, © Wayne Lynch/All Canada Photos/Alamy; 23TR, © FloridaStock/Shutterstock; 23BL, © Michio Hoshino/Minden Pictures/FLPA; 23BC, © Jurgen Freund/Nature Picture Library; 23BR, © Don Land/Shutterstock.

Publisher: Kenn Goin
Senior Editor: Joyce Tavolacci
Creative Director: Spencer Brinker
Photo Researcher: Ruby Tuesday Ltd

Library of Congress Cataloging-in-Publication Data

Phillips, Dee, 1967– author.
  Harp seal / by Dee Phillips.
      pages cm. — (Arctic animals)
  Includes bibliographical references and index.
  ISBN 978-1-62724-531-9 (library binding) — ISBN 1-62724-531-6 (library binding)
  1. Harp seal—Juvenile literature. I. Title.
  QL737.P64P476 2015
  599.79'29—dc23
                            2014035743

For more information, write to Bearport Publishing Company, Inc., 45 West 21st Street, Suite 3B, New York, New York 10010. Printed in the United States of America.

10 9 8 7 6 5 4 3 2 1

Contents

Time for Breakfast

It's a spring morning in the **Arctic**—one of the coldest places on Earth.

A fluffy, white baby harp seal waits on the sea ice beside a hole.

Suddenly, its mother pops up from the hole.

The mother seal has been swimming in the ocean.

Now she climbs out of the hole to feed her hungry pup some milk.

the Arctic

In the Arctic, it can be colder than the inside of a freezer. A harp seal pup isn't protected by a cozy home, though. The baby seal lives and sleeps on the ice.

harp seal pup

mother harp seal

An Icy Ocean Home

Harp seals live in the Arctic Ocean and the North Atlantic Ocean.

These oceans are very cold and icy.

Adult harp seals spend nearly all their time in the chilly waters.

Sometimes they climb onto huge pieces of floating ice.

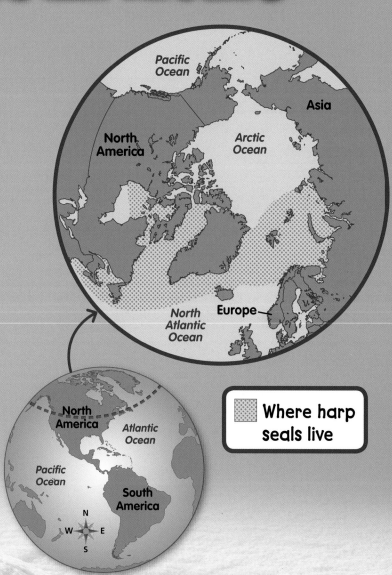

Pacific Ocean

Asia

North America

Arctic Ocean

North Atlantic Ocean

Europe

North America

Atlantic Ocean

Pacific Ocean

South America

N E S W

Where harp seals live

An adult harp seal can fall asleep while floating in the ocean.

adult harp seals on floating ice

What kinds of food do you think an adult harp seal eats?

A Seafood Dinner

An adult harp seal spends lots of time looking for food.

It catches and eats fish and shrimp.

While feeding, it may dive up to 1,300 feet (396 m).

The seal can stay underwater for about 15 minutes.

Then the seal swims back up to the water's surface to breathe air.

fish

shrimp

adult harp seal underwater

An adult harp seal can be up to 6 feet (1.8 m) long. It can weigh up to 300 pounds (136 kg). That's nearly as much as two adult humans!

How do you think a harp seal stays warm in the ice-cold water?

Keeping Warm

A harp seal has a thick layer of fat underneath its skin.

This fat is called **blubber**.

It keeps the seal warm in the ice-cold ocean.

An adult harp seal also has a coat of silvery-gray fur.

If a seal leaves the water, its fur helps keep it warm in the cold Arctic air.

In spring, adult seals rest on floating ice for several weeks. During this time, the seals **molt**. This means their old, worn-out furry coat falls out and a new coat grows in.

silvery-gray fur

Time for Pups

In late spring, a male and female harp seal meet up in the ocean to **mate**.

The next spring, the female seal gives birth to a pup on a chunk of floating ice.

The little pup has a thick coat of yellowish-white fur.

The fur keeps the baby warm in its freezing Arctic home.

harp seal mothers and pups

Lots of female seals gather together to give birth. Sometimes there may be as many as 2,000 pairs of mothers and pups on the same piece of ice.

one-day-old
harp seal pup

How would you describe a
harp seal pup to someone
who has never seen one?

13

Staying Safe

About three days after the pup is born, its coat turns bright white.

Now the baby seal blends in with the ice and snow.

This helps keep the pup safe from polar bears.

These large **predators** eat baby seals.

The pup's white **camouflage** makes it harder for polar bears to see it.

polar bear

Adult harp seals also have enemies. Polar bears may attack them on the ice. In the ocean, killer whales and sharks hunt adult seals.

five-day-old harp seal pup

Baby Food

A harp seal pup drinks milk from its mother's body.

The milk is thick and full of fat.

It helps the little pup's body make lots of blubber.

When the mother seal is hungry, she leaves the baby.

She finds a hole in the ice and slides into the water to go hunting.

a pup waits on the ice while its mother goes hunting

A harp seal pup weighs about 25 pounds (11 kg) when it is born. Its mother's fatty milk helps it grow bigger and heavier very quickly. In fact, the pup gains about 5 pounds (2 kg) each day.

pup drinking milk

A pup weighs 25 pounds (11 kg). If it gains 5 pounds (2 kg) each day for five days, how much will it weigh?

(The answer is on page 24.)

17

Growing Up

When a harp seal is only 12 days old, it is ready to live on its own.

The mother seal goes back to live in the ocean.

The pup stays on the ice for about three more weeks.

During this time, its fluffy white coat falls out.

A new thick gray coat with dark spots grows.

twelve-day-old harp seal pup

A female harp seal usually has her first pup when she is five or six years old. Harp seals live for 20 to 30 years.

four-week-old pup

new gray spotty coat

old white fur

Into the Ocean

After a while, the pup's new spotted coat has grown in.

Then the young seal finds a hole in the ice and slides into the water.

It has not had anything to eat for several weeks.

The hungry pup swims underwater and catches fish and shrimp.

Now the pup is ready to begin its life in the sea!

five-week-old seal pup

seal pup in the ocean

Over the next three years, the young seal's spotty coat turns pale gray. The grown-up seal looks just like its mother.

three-year-old harp seal

Adult harp seals have dark patches of fur on their backs. In a notebook, draw a picture of an adult harp seal.

Science Lab

Make a Blubber Glove

A harp seal's blubber keeps it warm in the icy ocean. Check out how blubber works in this activity.

> **You will need:**
> • A mixing bowl • Water • Ice cubes
> • Two medium-sized clear plastic bags • A spoon
> • Enough vegetable shortening to fill one bag

1. Fill a mixing bowl with cold water and lots of ice cubes.

2. Put your left hand in the ice water for about 30 seconds.

   How does your hand feel?

3. Now use a spoon to fill one bag with shortening. Put your right hand inside the clean, empty bag and push it into the shortening-filled bag.

Do you think this hand will feel colder, warmer, or the same if you put it into the ice water?

4. Test your prediction by putting your right hand into the ice water for about 30 seconds.

   How does this hand feel? Did what happened match your prediction? What is happening to the hand inside the bag filled with shortening?

(The answers are on page 24.)

Science Words

Arctic (ARK-tik) the northernmost area on Earth, which includes the Arctic Ocean and the North Pole

blubber (BLUH-bur) a layer of fat under the skin of animals such as seals and whales

camouflage (KAM-uh-flazh) the colors and markings on an animal that help it blend in with its surroundings

mate (MAYT) to come together in order to have young

molt (MOHLT) to shed an old coat of fur and grow a new one

predators (PRED-uh-turz) animals that hunt and eat other animals

23

Index

Read More

Drumlin, Sam. *Harp Seals (Sea Friends)*. New York: PowerKids Press (2013).

Owen, Ruth. *Seal Pups (Water Babies)*. New York: Bearport (2013).

Townsend, Emily Rose. *Seals (Polar Animals)*. North Mankato, MN: Capstone (2006).

Learn More Online

To learn more about harp seals, visit **www.bearportpublishingcom/ArcticAnimals**

About the Author

Dee Phillips lives near the ocean on the southwest coast of England. She develops and writes nonfiction and fiction books for children of all ages.

Answers

Page 17: The pup will weigh 50 pounds (22 kg).

Page 22: The hand inside the bag filled with shortening is insulated, or protected, from the icy water. It feels less cold than the uncovered hand. The shortening acts like a seal's blubber, which insulates the seal's body against icy water.